Contents

Acknowledgments
'Five little speckled frogs' by L B Scott and V Pavelko (usually 'Ten little frogs') is reproduced by permission of Belwin-Mills Publishing Corporation (© 1954 Bowmar Noble) and International Music Publications.

British Library Cataloguing in Publication Data

Counting songs.—(Action rhymes. Series no. 8815).
   1. children's counting out rhymes in English — Anthologies
   I. Finnigan, Helen   II. Langton, Roger
398'.8

ISBN 0-7214-1123-1

First edition

Published by Ladybird Books Ltd Loughborough Leicestershire UK
Ladybird Books Inc Auburn Maine 04210 USA

Ladybird Action Rhymes

Counting songs

compiled by Helen Finnigan
illustrated by Roger Langton

Ladybird Books

Three blind mice,
Three blind mice,
See how they run,
See how they run!

They all run after the farmer's wife,
Who cuts off their tails with a carving knife,
Did ever you see such a thing in your life,
As three blind mice?

Baa, baa, black sheep,
Have you any wool?
Yes, sir, yes, sir,
Three bags full.

One for the master,
And one for the dame,
And one for the little boy
Who lives down the lane.

I saw three ships come sailing by,
Sailing by,
Sailing by,
I saw three ships come sailing by,
On Christmas Day in the morning.

And what do you think was in them then,
Was in them then,
Was in them then,
And what do you think was in them then,
On Christmas Day in the morning?

Three pretty girls were in them then,
Were in them then,
Were in them then,
Three pretty girls were in them then,
On Christmas Day in the morning.

One could whistle and one could sing
And one could play
On the violin,
Such joy there was at my wedding,
On Christmas Day in the morning.

Johnny taps with one hammer,
One hammer, one hammer.
Johnny taps with one hammer,
Then he taps with two.

Johnny taps with two hammers,
Two hammers, two hammers.
Johnny taps with two hammers,
Then he taps with three.

Johnny taps with three hammers,
Three hammers, three hammers.
Johnny taps with three hammers,
Then he taps with four.

Johnny taps with four hammers,
Four hammers, four hammers.
Johnny taps with four hammers,
Then he taps with five.

Johnny taps with five hammers,
Five hammers, five hammers.
Johnny taps with five hammers,
Then he goes on strike.

When Goldilocks went to the house
  of the bears,
O, what did her blue eyes see?
A bowl that was huge,
A bowl that was small,
And a bowl that was tiny,
And that was all.
She counted them one, two, three.

When Goldilocks went to the house
   of the bears,
O, what did her blue eyes see?
A chair that was huge,
A chair that was small,
A chair that was tiny,
And that was all.
She counted them,
   one, two, three.

When Goldilocks went to the house
   of the bears,
O, what did her blue eyes see?
A bed that was huge,
A bed that was small,
A bed that was tiny,
And that was all.
She counted them, one, two, three.

When Goldilocks ran from the house
   of the bears,
O, what did her blue eyes see?
A bear that was huge,
A bear that was small,
A bear that was tiny,
And that was all.
They growled at her, grr, grr, grr.

Five little ducks went swimming one day,
Over the pond and far away.
Mother duck said, "Quack, quack, quack, quack."
But only four little ducks came back.

Four little ducks went swimming one day,
Over the pond and far away.
Mother duck said, "Quack, quack, quack, quack."
But only three little ducks came back.

Three little ducks went swimming one day,
Over the pond and far away.
Mother duck said, "Quack, quack, quack, quack."
But only two little ducks came back.

Two little ducks went swimming one day,
Over the pond and far away.
Mother duck said, "Quack, quack, quack, quack."
But only one little duck came back.

One little duck went swimming one day,
Over the pond and far away.
Daddy duck said, "Quack, quack, quack, quack."
And five little ducks came swimming back.

Five little speckled frogs,
Sat on a speckled log,
Catching some most delicious bugs.
     Yum, yum.
One jumped into the pool,
Where it was nice and cool,
Then there were four green speckled frogs.
     Glub, glub.

Four little speckled frogs,
Sat on a speckled log,
Catching some most delicious bugs.
     Yum, yum.
One jumped into the pool,
Where it was nice and cool,
Then there were three green speckled frogs.
     Glub, glub.

Three little speckled frogs,
Sat on a speckled log,
Catching some most
                    delicious bugs.
    Yum, yum.
One jumped into the pool,
Where it was nice and cool,
Then there were two green
                    speckled frogs.
    Glub, glub.

Two little speckled frogs,
Sat on a speckled log,
Catching some most delicious bugs.
    Yum, yum.
One jumped into the pool,
Where it was nice and cool,
Then there was one green speckled frog.
    Glub, glub.

One little speckled frog,
Sat on a speckled log,
Catching some most delicious bugs.
    Yum, yum.
He jumped into the pool,
Where it was nice and cool,
Then there were no green speckled frogs.
    Glub, glub.

Five currant buns in a baker's shop,
Round and fat with sugar on the top.
Along came a boy with a penny one day,
Bought a currant bun and took it away.

Four currant buns in a baker's shop,
Round and fat with sugar on the top.
Along came a boy with a penny one day,
Bought a currant bun and took it away.

Three currant buns, etc.

Two currant buns, etc.

One currant bun, etc.

One little finger,
One little finger,
One little finger,
Tap, tap, tap.
Point to the ceiling,
Point to the floor,
And lay it in your
                    lap, lap, lap.

Two little fingers,
Two little fingers,
Two little fingers,
Tap, tap, tap.
Point to the ceiling,
Point to the floor,
And lay them in your
                    lap, lap, lap.

Three little fingers,
Three little fingers,
Three little fingers,
Tap, tap, tap.
Point to the ceiling,
Point to the floor,
And lay them in your
                    lap, lap, lap.

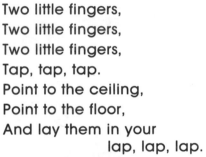

Four little fingers, etc.

Five little fingers, etc.

Bell horses, bell horses,
What time of day?
One o'clock, two o'clock,
Three and away.

Bell horses, bell horses,
What time of day?
Two o'clock, three o'clock,
Four and away.

Bell horses, bell horses,
What time of day?
Five o'clock, six o'clock,
Now time to stay.

Six little ducks that I once knew,
Fat ducks, pretty ducks, they were too.

Chorus
But the one little duck with the feather
   on his back,
He led the others with his quack,
   quack, quack.
Quack, quack, quack,
   quack, quack, quack.
He led the others with his quack,
   quack, quack.

Down to the river they would go,
Wibble wobble, wibble wobble, to and fro.
Chorus

Into the river he would dive,
Over and under the other five.
Chorus

Home from the river they would come,
Wibble wobble, wibble wobble,
   ho, hum hum.
Chorus

One day as sure as you're alive,
More ducks will follow the other five.
Chorus

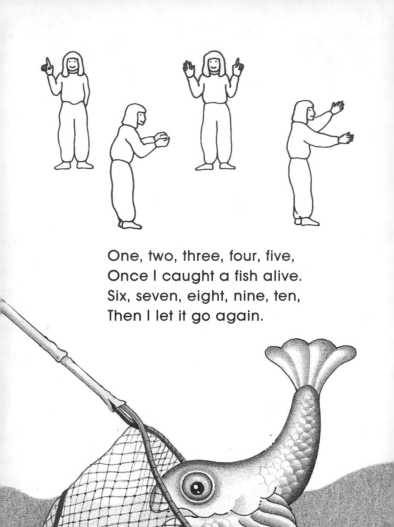

One, two, three, four, five,
Once I caught a fish alive.
Six, seven, eight, nine, ten,
Then I let it go again.

Why did you let it go?
Because it bit my finger so.
Which finger did it bite?
This little finger on the right.

Ten green bottles hanging on the wall,
Ten green bottles hanging on the wall,
And if one green bottle should accidentally fall
There'd be nine green bottles hanging on the wall.

Nine green bottles hanging on the wall,
Nine green bottles hanging on the wall,
And if one green bottle should accidentally fall
There'd be eight green bottles hanging on the wall.

Eight green bottles hanging on the wall,
Eight green bottles hanging on the wall,
And if one green bottle should accidentally fall
There'd be seven green bottles hanging on the wall.

Seven green bottles, etc, down to

One green bottle hanging on the wall,
One green bottle hanging on the wall,
And if that green bottle should accidentally fall
There'd be no green bottles hanging there at all.

John Brown had a little soldier,
John Brown had a little soldier,
John Brown had a little soldier,
One little soldier boy.
He had one little, two little, three little soldiers,
Four little, five little, six little soldiers,
Seven little, eight little, nine little soldiers,
Ten little soldier boys.   *Hoy*

John Brown had ten little soldiers,
John Brown had ten little soldiers,
John Brown had ten little soldiers,
Ten little soldier boys.
He had ten little, nine little, eight little soldiers,
Seven little, six little, five little soldiers,
Four little, three little, two little soldiers,
One little soldier boy.   *Hoy*

This old man, he played one,
He played nick-nack on my drum.

Chorus
Nick-nack paddy whack,
Give a dog a bone,
This old man came rolling home.

This old man, he played two,
He played nick-nack on my shoe.
Chorus

This old man, he played three,
He played nick-nack on my knee.
Chorus

This old man, he played four,
He played nick-nack on my door.
Chorus

This old man, he played five,
He played nick-nack on my hive.
Chorus

This old man, he played six,
He played nick-nack on my sticks.
Chorus

This old man, he played seven,
He played nick-nack up in Heaven.
Chorus

This old man, he played eight,
He played nick-nack on my plate.
Chorus

This old man, he played nine,
He played nick-nack on my line.
Chorus

This old man, he played ten,
He played nick-nack on my hen.
Chorus

There were ten in the bed,
And the little one said,
"Roll over! Roll over!"
So they all rolled over,
And one fell out.

There were nine in the bed, etc.

There were eight in the bed, etc,

down to
There was one in the bed,
And the little one said,
"Roll over! Roll over!"
So he rolled right over and fell right out.

There were none in the bed, so no one said,
"Roll over! Roll over!"

One man went to mow,
Went to mow a meadow,
One man and his dog,
Went to mow a meadow.

Two men went to mow,
Went to mow a meadow,
Two men, one man and his dog,
Went to mow a meadow.

Three men went to mow,
Went to mow a meadow,
Three men, two men, one man and his dog,
Went to mow a meadow.

Four men went to mow, etc.

Five men went to mow, etc.

There were ten fat sausages sizzling in the pan,
One went 'POP!' and another went 'BANG!'

There were eight fat sausages sizzling in
   the pan,
One went 'POP!' and another went 'BANG!'

There were six fat sausages sizzling in the pan,
One went 'POP!' and another went 'BANG!'

There were four fat sausages, etc.

One, two,
   buckle my shoe.

Three, four,
   knock at the door.

Five, six,
   pick up sticks.

Seven, eight,
   lay them straight.

Nine, ten,
   a big fat hen.

Eleven, twelve,
dig and delve.

Thirteen, fourteen,
maids a-courting.

Fifteen, sixteen,
maids in the kitchen.

Seventeen, eighteen,
maids a-waiting.

Nineteen, twenty,
my plate's empty.

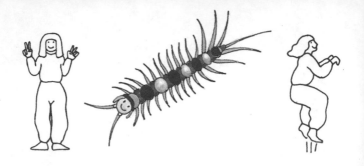

The animals came in two by two,
There's one more river to cross.
The centipede with the kangaroo,
There's one more river to cross.

Chorus
One more river, and that's the river of Jordan,
One more river, there's one more river to cross.

The animals came in three by three,
There's one more river to cross.
The elephant on the back of the flea,
There's one more river to cross.
Chorus

The animals came in four by four,
There's one more river to cross.
The camel he got stuck in the door,
There's one more river to cross.
Chorus

The animals came in five by five,
There's one more river to cross.
Some were dead, and some were alive.
There's one more river to cross.
Chorus

The animals came in six by six, *etc.*
The monkey he was up to his tricks, *etc.*
Chorus

The animals came in seven by seven, *etc.*
Some went to Hell, and some went to Heaven,
Chorus   *etc.*

The animals came in eight by eight, *etc.*
The worm was early, the bird was late, *etc.*
Chorus

The animals came in nine by nine, *etc.*
Some had water and some had wine, *etc.*
Chorus

The animals came in ten by ten,
        There's one more river to cross.
If you want any more you must sing it again,
        There's one more river to cross.

Chorus
One more river, and that's the river of Jordan,
One more river, there's one more river to cross.

One elephant went out to play,
Upon a spider's web one day.
He found it such enormous fun,
That he called for another elephant to come.

*One child is chosen as the first elephant and he
chooses a second child at the end of the first verse.
The second child then chooses a third, and so on.*

Over in the meadow in a snug beehive
   lived an old mother bee
   and her little bees five.
"Buzz," said the mother.
"We buzz," said the five.
So they buzzed all day long in a snug beehive.
Buzz – buzz – buzz.

Over in the meadow by the old barn door
   lived an old mother mouse
   and her little mice four.
"Squeak," said the mother.
"We squeak," said the four.
So they squeaked all day long
   by the old barn door.
Squeak – squeak – squeak.

Over in the meadow in a nest in a tree
   lived an old mother bird
   and her little birdies three.
"Chirp," said the mother.
"We chirp," said the three.
So they chirped all day long
   in a nest in a tree.
Chirp – chirp – chirp.

40

Over in the meadow where the oak tree grew
   lived an old mother chipmunk
   and her little chipmunks two.
"Dig," said the mother.
"We dig," said the two.
So they dug all day long
   where the oak tree grew.
Dig – dig – dig.

Over in the meadow where the deep waters run
   lived an old mother beaver
   and her little beaver one.
"Gnaw," said the mother.
"I gnaw," said the one.
So he gnawed all day long
   where the deep waters run.
Gnaw – gnaw – gnaw.

Note: The birthday child stands in the middle of a circle formed by his friends. He has a ring on one of his fingers.

Friends – How old are you?
          I'm five today.
(The friends now walk round singing.)

How old are you, my pretty little thing
With a ring upon your finger?
One or two, double you?
Three or four, more and more?
Five, six, seven, eight, nine, ten,
You are ladies or gentlemen.
How old are you, my pretty little thing,
With a ring upon your finger?

RECITATION (friends stand still)

If you're one – you are young.
If you're two – double you.
If you're three – wait and see.
If you're four – more and more.

Then they sing:
You are five, bees in a hive,
With a ring upon your finger.

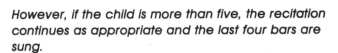

However, if the child is more than five, the recitation continues as appropriate and the last four bars are sung.

For example, for an 11th birthday,
If you're six – tock ticks.
If you're seven – Earth and Heaven.
If you're eight – do not wait.
If you're nine – just in time.
If you're ten – maids and men.

Sing:
You are eleven, four and seven
With a ring upon your finger.